CONTENTS

INTRODUCTION

Welcome to "The Wishpond Lead Generation Guide". In today's highly competitive business landscape, generating high-quality leads has become a crucial factor in driving sustainable growth and achieving long-term success.

Whether you are a seasoned marketer or a budding entrepreneur, understanding the art and science of lead generation is essential to thrive in the digital age. This comprehensive guide is designed to equip you with the knowledge, strategies, and practical insights needed to attract, engage, and convert your target audience into valuable leads.

Throughout these pages, we will explore the fundamental principles, proven tactics, and innovative techniques that empower you to create a robust lead generation ecosystem. From leveraging the power of social media and email marketing to optimizing landing pages and crafting compelling offers, we will dive deep into the core elements that drive successful lead generation campaigns.

But effective lead generation is more than just a collection of isolated tactics. It requires a holistic approach that integrates various elements seamlessly, aligning them with your business goals and audience's needs. That's why we will also focus on the importance of understanding your target market, conducting thorough audience research, and leveraging data-driven insights to inform your lead generation strategies.

As we embark on this journey together, we will also explore the rapidly evolving landscape of digital marketing and emerging trends that can impact your lead generation efforts. With technology advancing at an unprecedented pace, it is vital to stay ahead of the curve, adapt to changes, and leverage innovative tools and platforms that can amplify your results.

We believe that every business, regardless of its size or industry, has the potential to generate a consistent stream of high-quality leads. By equipping yourself with the knowledge and practical know-how shared within these pages, you will be empowered to unlock new opportunities, forge deeper connections with your prospects, and ultimately drive sustainable growth for your business.

So, whether you are looking to revamp your existing lead generation strategies or starting from scratch, "The Wishpond Lead Generation Guide" is your go-to resource. Get ready to embark on an exciting journey filled with actionable insights, expert advice, and real-world examples that will empower you to take your lead generation efforts to the next level.

Now, let's dive in and unlock the power of Wishpond for transforming your business's lead generation landscape. Your journey towards success starts here!

CHAPTER ONE

Introduction

Overview of lead generation in web-based business arrangements

In the fast-paced world of online business, lead generation plays a crucial role in attracting potential customers and converting them into loyal clients. Web-based business arrangements have revolutionized the way companies generate leads by utilizing the power of the internet. This overview aims to shed light on the fundamental aspects of lead generation in web-based business arrangements and how it can benefit companies in reaching their sales goals.

Definition of Lead Generation:

Lead generation refers to the process of identifying and cultivating potential customers for a business's products or services. In the context of web-based business arrangements, lead generation primarily involves leveraging online platforms and marketing techniques to attract individuals who are likely to be interested in what the business has to offer.

Channels for Lead Generation:

There are numerous channels through which lead generation can be achieved in web-based business arrangements. These include search engine optimization

(SEO), content marketing, social media marketing, email marketing, paid advertisements, influencer collaborations, and more. Each channel has its own unique benefits and target audience, allowing businesses to diversify their lead generation efforts.

Capturing Leads:

One of the primary goals of lead generation is to capture potential customers' contact information, such as their email addresses or phone numbers. This is typically done through lead capture forms or landing pages, where visitors are enticed to provide their details in exchange for valuable content or exclusive offers. These captured leads become a valuable asset for businesses, as they can be nurtured and eventually converted into paying customers.

Lead Nurturing:

Lead generation is not solely about capturing contact information; it also involves nurturing leads through strategic communication and relationship building. Once a business has obtained a lead's contact details, they can engage with them through personalized emails, targeted content, or social media interactions. This ongoing interaction helps to establish trust, showcase the business's expertise, and guide leads towards making a purchase decision.

Conversion Optimization:

The ultimate goal of lead generation is to convert leads into customers. Conversion optimization strategies focus on enhancing the likelihood of leads taking the desired action, such as making a purchase or signing up for a service. This involves optimizing website design, creating compelling calls-to-action, providing a seamless user experience, and employing persuasive copywriting techniques.

Measurement and Analytics:

To evaluate the effectiveness of lead generation efforts in web-based business arrangements, it is crucial to track and measure key performance indicators (KPIs). Tools like Google Analytics and marketing automation software provide valuable insights into metrics such as conversion rates, website traffic sources, email open rates, and more. These analytics enable businesses to refine their lead generation strategies and allocate resources effectively.

Importance Of Effective Lead Generation Strategies

Effective lead generation strategies are vital for the success and growth of any business. Without a consistent stream of qualified leads, a company may struggle to generate revenue, expand its customer base, or stay ahead of the competition. Let's explore the key reasons why implementing effective lead generation strategies is of utmost importance.

Increased Sales Opportunities:

Lead generation serves as a foundation for increasing sales opportunities. By capturing leads and nurturing them through the sales funnel, businesses can create a pipeline of potential customers who are more likely to convert. With a well-designed lead generation strategy in place, companies can identify and target individuals who have already shown interest in their products or services, increasing the chances of closing sales.

Cost-Effective Marketing:

Compared to traditional marketing methods, lead generation strategies in web-based business arrangements can be highly cost-effective. Digital marketing channels often provide a higher return on investment (ROI) due to their ability to target specific demographics and track performance metrics accurately. By focusing on lead generation efforts, businesses can optimize their marketing budgets and allocate resources where they are most likely to yield results.

Targeted Audience Engagement:

Effective lead generation strategies allow businesses to engage with a targeted audience that has expressed interest in their industry or offerings. This targeted approach ensures that marketing efforts are directed towards individuals who are more likely to convert into customers. By tailoring content and messaging to the needs and preferences of the target audience, businesses can build stronger relationships, establish trust, and increase the likelihood of conversions.

Competitive Advantage:

In today's competitive business landscape, companies need to stay ahead of their rivals. Implementing effective lead generation strategies can give businesses a significant competitive advantage. By effectively capturing and nurturing leads, companies can build a loyal customer base, establish themselves as industry leaders, and differentiate themselves from competitors who may be lagging behind in their lead generation efforts.

Business Growth and Expansion:

Lead generation is crucial for business growth and expansion. By consistently attracting and converting leads, businesses can expand their customer base, increase revenue, and explore new market opportunities. Effective lead generation strategies provide a scalable and sustainable approach to fueling business growth, allowing companies to tap into new markets and diversify their revenue streams.

How This Guide Will Help Businesses Optimize Lead Generation

This comprehensive guide aims to help businesses optimize their lead generation efforts and achieve better results in web-based business arrangements. By following the strategies and insights provided, companies can enhance their lead generation capabilities and maximize their return on investment. Here's how this guide can assist businesses:

In-Depth Understanding:

The guide provides a deep understanding of lead generation in web-based business arrangements. It covers the key concepts, channels, and techniques involved in effective lead generation, ensuring that businesses have a solid foundation of knowledge to build upon.

Proven Strategies:

The guide presents proven strategies and best practices for lead generation. These strategies have been tried and tested by industry experts and successful businesses. By implementing these strategies, companies can leverage the experience of others and increase the effectiveness of their lead generation initiatives.

Step-by-Step Implementation:

The guide offers a step-by-step approach to implementing lead generation strategies. It breaks down the process into manageable steps, allowing businesses to follow along and take action. From optimizing website design to crafting compelling content, the guide provides practical advice for each stage of the lead generation journey.

Optimization Techniques:

In addition to the initial implementation, the guide also focuses on optimization techniques. It provides insights into how businesses can continually improve their lead generation efforts by analyzing data, identifying bottlenecks, and making data-driven decisions. Optimization is crucial for long-term success in lead generation, and this guide equips businesses with the knowledge to achieve it.

Real-Life Examples:

To illustrate the concepts and strategies discussed, the guide includes real-life examples from successful businesses. These examples demonstrate how lead generation strategies have been applied in various industries and provide inspiration for businesses looking to optimize their own lead generation processes.

By leveraging the knowledge and insights provided in this guide, businesses can enhance their lead generation capabilities and drive sustainable growth in web-based business arrangements. Whether it's attracting more qualified leads, improving conversion rates, or staying ahead of the competition, optimizing lead generation is a crucial component of any successful online business.

Understanding Web-Based Business Arrangements

Definition and types of web-based business arrangements

Web-based business arrangements refer to the various ways in which businesses utilize the internet and digital technologies to conduct their operations, reach customers, and generate revenue. These arrangements leverage the power of online platforms and connectivity to establish a presence, facilitate transactions, and engage with a wide audience. Let's explore the definition and types of web-based business arrangements in more detail.

Definition of Web-based Business Arrangements:

Web-based business arrangements encompass any business model or framework that heavily relies on internet technologies and online platforms to carry out its operations. These arrangements can range from e-commerce stores selling products online to service-based businesses offering virtual consultations or remote services. The common thread among these arrangements is the utilization of digital channels as the primary means of conducting business activities.

Types of Web-based Business Arrangements:

    a. E-commerce: E-commerce refers to the buying and selling of goods or services over the internet. This includes online retail stores, marketplaces, and platforms where transactions are conducted electronically. E-commerce businesses leverage web-based technologies to showcase products, manage inventory, process payments, and handle order fulfillment.

b. Software as a Service (SaaS): SaaS is a web-based business arrangement where software applications are delivered over the internet on a subscription basis. Instead of purchasing and installing software locally, users access and use the software through a web browser. SaaS businesses provide cloud-based solutions for various purposes, such as project management, customer relationship management (CRM), and accounting.

c. Online Marketplaces: Online marketplaces serve as platforms where multiple sellers can list and sell their products or services to a broad customer base. Examples include Amazon, eBay, and Etsy. These web-based business arrangements provide a centralized platform for buyers and sellers to connect, facilitating transactions and streamlining the buying process.

d. Content-Based Businesses: Content-based businesses focus on creating and delivering valuable content to attract and engage an audience. This can include blogs, news websites, online magazines, and video platforms like YouTube. These arrangements generate revenue through advertising, sponsored content, subscriptions, or a combination of different monetization strategies.

e. Online Booking and Reservation Systems: Businesses in the hospitality, travel, and service industries often rely on web-based booking and reservation systems. These arrangements allow customers to book accommodations, flights, restaurants, appointments, and other services online. Examples include hotel booking platforms like Booking.com and restaurant reservation systems like OpenTable.

f. Online Learning and Education: With the rise of digital learning, web-based arrangements in the education sector have gained significant traction. Online learning platforms and educational websites provide courses, tutorials, and educational resources to learners of all ages. These arrangements enable remote learning, self-paced education, and access to a global network of educators and students.

Advantages And Challenges Of Web-Based Business Models

Web-based business models offer several advantages that have propelled their rapid growth and adoption in various industries. However, they also come with their fair share of challenges. Understanding both the advantages and challenges is essential for businesses considering or already operating within web-based business models.

Advantages:

- Global Reach: One of the significant advantages of web-based business models is their potential to reach a global audience. By leveraging the internet, businesses can transcend geographical boundaries and tap into a vast pool of potential customers. This global reach opens up new markets and revenue streams, providing opportunities for business growth and expansion.
- Lower Costs: Web-based business models often offer cost-saving benefits compared to traditional brick-and-mortar operations. Online businesses can avoid expenses associated with physical retail spaces, such as rent, utilities, and maintenance. Additionally, digital marketing and advertising methods can be more cost-effective than traditional marketing channels, allowing businesses to allocate their budgets more efficiently.
- Increased Flexibility: Web-based business models provide greater flexibility in terms of working hours and location. Entrepreneurs and employees

can work remotely, manage their schedules, and reach customers at any time, enhancing work-life balance and accommodating diverse lifestyles. This flexibility can also attract and retain talented individuals who value autonomy and freedom in their work.

- Data-driven Decision Making: Web-based business models generate a wealth of data that can be leveraged for informed decision making. Through web analytics, businesses can gain insights into customer behavior, preferences, and purchasing patterns. This data can guide marketing strategies, product development, and customer relationship management, leading to more effective and targeted business operations.

Challenges:

- Intense Competition: The ease of entry into web-based business models has led to intense competition in many industries. With low barriers to entry, businesses must distinguish themselves from competitors to attract and retain customers. Building a strong brand, providing exceptional customer experiences, and continuously innovating are crucial for success in a highly competitive online marketplace.
- Cybersecurity Risks: Web-based business models face inherent cybersecurity risks due to the nature of online transactions and data storage. Businesses must invest in robust security measures to protect customer data, prevent unauthorized access, and defend against cyber threats. Failure to prioritize cybersecurity can lead

to reputational damage, legal issues, and loss of customer trust.

- Technological Dependence: Web-based business models heavily rely on technology infrastructure and internet connectivity. Dependence on these factors introduces the risk of technical failures, server outages, or connectivity issues. Downtime or technical glitches can disrupt business operations, impact customer experience, and result in revenue loss. Businesses must invest in reliable infrastructure and contingency plans to mitigate these risks.

- Digital Marketing Complexity: While digital marketing provides opportunities for effective targeting and cost-efficient campaigns, it also presents challenges. The digital landscape is constantly evolving, requiring businesses to stay updated with new technologies, algorithms, and platforms. Maintaining a strong online presence and effectively navigating digital marketing channels often requires specialized knowledge or the support of digital marketing experts.

Target Audience Analysis And Identification

Target audience analysis and identification are essential steps in developing successful marketing and business strategies. Understanding who your target audience is enables businesses to tailor their messaging, products, and services to meet their needs and preferences. Let's explore the significance of target audience analysis and identification in more detail.

Definition of Target Audience:

The target audience refers to a specific group of individuals or businesses that a company aims to reach, engage, and sell its products or services to. This group shares common characteristics, interests, demographics, and behaviors that make them more likely to be interested in what the business has to offer.

Importance of Target Audience Analysis:

Target audience analysis helps businesses make informed decisions about marketing strategies, product development, and customer engagement. It allows companies to understand the motivations, preferences, and pain points of their target audience, enabling them to create tailored solutions and impactful marketing campaigns. By aligning their efforts with the needs of the target audience, businesses can increase customer satisfaction and drive sales growth.

Steps in Target Audience Analysis:

- Market Research: Conducting comprehensive market research is the first step in target audience analysis. This involves gathering data on industry trends, competitor analysis, and customer insights. Market research helps identify gaps in the market, understand customer expectations, and determine the competitive landscape.

- Demographic Analysis: Demographic analysis involves examining the key demographic factors of the target audience, such as age, gender, location, income level, education, and occupation. These factors provide valuable insights into the target audience's purchasing power, lifestyle preferences, and buying behaviors.
- Psychographic Analysis: Psychographic analysis delves into the psychological and emotional aspects of the target audience. It explores their attitudes, values, interests, hobbies, and lifestyle choices. Psychographic analysis helps businesses understand the target audience's motivations, aspirations, and the underlying factors that drive their purchasing decisions.
- Behavioral Analysis: Behavioral analysis focuses on understanding the target audience's actions and behaviors. It examines their purchasing patterns, online behaviors, brand interactions, and response to marketing campaigns. Behavioral analysis helps identify opportunities for customer engagement and personalized marketing approaches.
- Customer Surveys and Feedback: Gathering direct feedback from existing customers through surveys, interviews, or feedback forms provides valuable insights into their experiences, preferences, and satisfaction levels. This feedback can uncover specific pain points, highlight areas

for improvement, and validate assumptions made during target audience analysis.

Benefits of Target Audience Identification:

Effective Messaging: Understanding the target audience enables businesses to craft compelling and relevant messaging that resonates with their potential customers. By speaking directly to their needs, aspirations, and pain points, businesses can capture attention and build meaningful connections.

Product Development: Target audience analysis informs product development by identifying gaps in the market and understanding the features and benefits that will appeal to the target audience. By tailoring products or services to meet their specific needs, businesses can gain a competitive edge and drive customer satisfaction.

Efficient Resource Allocation: Identifying the target audience helps businesses allocate their resources effectively. By focusing marketing efforts on the channels and platforms preferred by the target audience, businesses can optimize their marketing budgets and maximize their return on investment.

Enhanced Customer Experience: When businesses understand their target audience, they can provide a more personalized and tailored customer experience. This includes offering relevant content, personalized recommendations, and efficient customer service. Enhanced customer experiences lead to increased customer loyalty and advocacy.

Target audience analysis and identification are ongoing processes. As markets evolve and consumer preferences change, businesses must continually gather data and refine their understanding of their target audience to stay ahead of the curve and adapt their strategies accordingly.

Defining Lead Generation

What is lead generation and why is it crucial?

Lead generation is the process of identifying and attracting potential customers (leads) who have shown interest in a business's products or services. It involves capturing their contact information, such as email addresses or phone numbers, to initiate further communication and nurture them towards becoming paying customers. Lead generation is crucial for several reasons:

- Expansion of Customer Base: Lead generation allows businesses to expand their customer base by reaching individuals who have expressed interest in their offerings. By capturing leads and nurturing them through the sales funnel, businesses increase their chances of converting them into paying customers, thereby growing their customer base.

- Revenue Generation: Leads are potential customers who are more likely to make a purchase compared to random website visitors. Effective lead generation strategies provide a steady stream of qualified leads, increasing the opportunity for sales conversions and revenue generation.

- Cost-Effective Marketing: Lead generation can be more cost-effective than traditional marketing methods. By targeting specific demographics and individuals who have already shown interest in the business's industry or offerings, businesses can allocate their marketing budgets more efficiently, resulting in a higher return on investment (ROI).

- Relationship Building: Lead generation is not only about capturing contact information; it also involves nurturing leads and building relationships. By engaging with leads through personalized communication, businesses can establish trust, showcase their expertise, and develop a rapport that increases the likelihood of converting leads into loyal customers.
- Market Research and Insights: Lead generation provides valuable market research and insights into customer behavior and preferences. By analyzing the data collected during lead generation efforts, businesses can gain a deeper understanding of their target audience, identify trends, and make data-driven decisions to refine their marketing strategies.

Differentiating Between Leads And Prospects

In the context of sales and marketing, leads and prospects are often used interchangeably. However, there is a subtle difference between the two:

- Leads: Leads are individuals or businesses who have expressed interest in a company's products or services by providing their contact information. They are potential customers who have taken a specific action that indicates their interest, such as filling out a lead capture form or subscribing to a newsletter. Leads are at an early stage in the sales process and require further nurturing to move them closer to a purchase decision.

- Prospects: Prospects are leads who have been qualified and identified as having a higher likelihood of becoming paying customers. They have passed through certain qualification criteria set by the business, such as having a specific budget, fitting certain demographic characteristics, or demonstrating a higher level of interest. Prospects have progressed further in the sales process and are considered more likely to convert into customers compared to general leads.

In summary, all prospects are leads, but not all leads are prospects. Leads represent a broader pool of individuals who have shown initial interest, while prospects are a subset of leads who have met specific criteria indicating a higher potential for conversion.

Key Components Of Successful Lead Generation

Successful lead generation relies on several key components that work together to attract and convert potential customers. Here are the essential components of a successful lead generation generatio

- Targeted Audience: Understanding the target audience is crucial for effective lead generation. Businesses need to identify their ideal customers, define their characteristics and preferences, and tailor their lead generation efforts to reach this specific audience.
- Compelling Offer: To entice potential customers to provide their contact information, businesses must offer something of value in return. This can include exclusive content, free resources, discounts, or access to special promotions. The offer should align with the target audience's interests and provide a clear benefit.
- Lead Capture Forms or Landing Pages: Lead capture forms or landing pages serve as the mechanism for collecting contact information from potential customers. These forms should be strategically placed on web pages and optimized for conversion, with clear and concise instructions and minimal barriers to entry.
- Quality Content: High-quality and relevant content is essential for attracting and engaging potential customers. Content can take the form of blog posts, articles, videos, infographics, or e-books. By providing valuable information,

businesses can position themselves as trusted industry authorities and capture leads who are seeking solutions or information related to their offerings.

- Multi-Channel Marketing: Effective lead generation strategies leverage multiple marketing channels to reach a broader audience. This can include search engine optimization (SEO) to drive organic traffic, social media marketing to engage with potential customers, email marketing to nurture leads, and paid advertising to expand reach and visibility.
- Lead Nurturing: Lead nurturing involves building relationships and engaging with leads to guide them through the sales funnel. This can be achieved through personalized email marketing campaigns, targeted content, and social media interactions. Lead nurturing aims to provide relevant information, address pain points, and establish trust, ultimately increasing the likelihood of conversion.
- Continuous Analysis and Optimization: Successful lead generation requires ongoing analysis and optimization. Businesses should regularly track and measure key performance indicators (KPIs) such as conversion rates, website traffic sources, and lead engagement. This data helps identify areas for improvement, optimize marketing strategies, and allocate resources effectively.

By implementing these key components and continuously refining their lead generation efforts, businesses can attract qualified leads, nurture them, and increase the likelihood of converting them into loyal customers.

CHAPTER TWO

*Crafting an Effective Lead
Generation Strategy*

Setting clear goals and objectives

Setting clear goals and objectives is a fundamental component of successful lead generation. Without clearly defined goals, businesses may struggle to develop effective strategies and measure their progress. Here's why setting clear goals and objectives is crucial:

- Focus and Direction: Goals provide businesses with a clear focus and direction. They establish what the business aims to achieve through lead generation efforts, whether it's increasing sales, expanding the customer base, or improving brand awareness. Clear goals help align efforts and resources towards achieving specific outcomes.
- Measurable Outcomes: Setting clear goals allows businesses to establish measurable outcomes and key performance indicators (KPIs). This enables them to track progress, evaluate the effectiveness of lead generation strategies, and make data-driven decisions based on real-time performance data.
- Motivation and Accountability: Goals serve as a source of motivation for teams and individuals

involved in lead generation. By setting specific and achievable goals, businesses create a sense of purpose and drive, increasing productivity and commitment. Goals also facilitate accountability, as they provide a benchmark against which performance can be evaluated.

- Resource Allocation: Clear goals help businesses allocate resources effectively. By understanding the desired outcomes, businesses can allocate budgets, time, and manpower accordingly. This ensures that resources are focused on activities that directly contribute to achieving lead generation goals.

- Alignment with Business Objectives: Setting goals for lead generation ensures alignment with broader business objectives. It helps businesses connect their lead generation efforts to the overall growth and success of the organization. By aligning goals, businesses ensure that lead generation strategies support the larger business strategy and contribute to long-term success.

Identifying Target Audience Preferences And Behaviors

Identifying the preferences and behaviors of the target audience is vital for successful lead generation. Understanding what motivates and influences potential customers allows businesses to tailor their strategies and messaging accordingly. Here's why it's crucial to identify target audience preferences and behaviors:

- Personalized Marketing: Target audience preferences and behaviors provide valuable insights for personalizing marketing efforts. By understanding their interests, needs, and pain points, businesses can create targeted and relevant content that resonates with potential customers. Personalized marketing increases the chances of capturing their attention, engaging them, and driving conversions.
- Effective Communication: Knowing the preferences and behaviors of the target audience helps businesses communicate in a way that resonates with them. It enables businesses to use the right tone, language, and messaging style that align with their preferences. Effective communication builds trust, establishes credibility, and encourages engagement with potential customers.
- Tailored Product Development: Understanding target audience preferences and behaviors helps inform product development strategies. By gaining insights into what potential customers value, businesses can create products or services

that meet their specific needs and preferences. Tailored product development increases the chances of attracting and converting potential customers into paying customers.

- Competitor Analysis: Identifying target audience preferences and behaviors also involves analyzing competitors' strategies. By understanding how competitors engage with the target audience, businesses can identify gaps, differentiation opportunities, and areas for improvement. This analysis helps businesses position themselves effectively and offer unique value propositions.

- Channel Selection: Preferences and behaviors of the target audience guide businesses in selecting the right marketing channels. Different target audiences may have varying preferences for communication and engagement. Some may prefer social media platforms, while others may respond better to email marketing or search engine optimization (SEO). Identifying these preferences helps businesses allocate resources to the most effective channels.

Utilizing Market Research For Data-Driven Strategies

Market research plays a crucial role in developing data-driven lead generation strategies. It involves gathering and analyzing data about the target market, competition, and consumer behavior. Here's why utilizing market research is essential for successful lead generation:

- Customer Insights: Market research provides valuable customer insights that help businesses understand their target audience. It uncovers demographic information, preferences, purchasing behavior, and pain points. This information allows businesses to create buyer personas and tailor lead generation strategies to address specific customer needs.
- Identifying Opportunities: Market research helps identify market gaps, trends, and emerging opportunities. By understanding the competitive landscape and consumer demands, businesses can spot untapped niches, identify unmet needs, and develop unique value propositions. This enables businesses to position themselves strategically and capitalize on market opportunities.
- Competitor Analysis: Market research involves analyzing competitors' strategies, strengths, and weaknesses. By understanding competitors' offerings, marketing tactics, and target audience engagement, businesses can differentiate themselves and offer unique value. Competitor analysis helps businesses identify gaps in the

market and develop strategies to gain a competitive edge.

- Validation and Refinement: Data-driven strategies rely on market research to validate assumptions and refine approaches. By testing hypotheses and analyzing market data, businesses can evaluate the effectiveness of their lead generation strategies. Market research provides insights into what works and what needs improvement, enabling businesses to refine their strategies based on empirical evidence.
- Effective Resource Allocation: Utilizing market research helps businesses allocate resources effectively. By understanding market dynamics, customer preferences, and competition, businesses can allocate budgets, time, and manpower to the most effective lead generation channels and tactics. This ensures efficient resource allocation and maximizes the return on investment (ROI).

In summary, market research provides businesses with valuable insights into the target audience, market opportunities, and competition. By utilizing market research, businesses can develop data-driven lead generation strategies that are more likely to attract and convert potential customers.

Optimizing Landing Pages And Conversion Paths

Designing compelling landing pages

Designing compelling landing pages is crucial for successful lead generation. A well-designed landing page can capture visitors' attention, engage them, and persuade them to take the desired action, such as filling out a lead capture form or making a purchase. Here are key considerations for designing compelling landing pages:

- Clear and Concise Messaging: The messaging on a landing page should be clear, concise, and focused on the key value proposition. It should clearly communicate the benefits of the offer or product and address the pain points of the target audience. Avoid cluttered or confusing content and ensure that the messaging is easy to understand.
- Compelling Headline: A strong headline grabs visitors' attention and conveys the main message or offer of the landing page. It should be concise, compelling, and communicate the value proposition succinctly. The headline should make visitors want to explore further and learn more about the offer.
- Engaging Visuals: Visual elements such as images, videos, or graphics can enhance the overall appeal and engagement of a landing page. Use high-quality visuals that are relevant to the offer or product being promoted. Visuals should be attention-grabbing, professional, and convey the desired emotions or benefits associated with the

offer.

- Simple and Intuitive Layout: The layout of a landing page should be clean, uncluttered, and easy to navigate. Use white space effectively to create a sense of balance and focus attention on key elements. Place important elements, such as the headline, call-to-action (CTA), and lead capture form, prominently and ensure they are easily accessible without excessive scrolling.
- Mobile-Friendly Design: With the increasing use of mobile devices, it is essential to design landing pages that are optimized for mobile viewing. Ensure that the landing page is responsive, loads quickly on mobile devices, and offers a seamless user experience. Mobile-friendly design increases accessibility and improves conversion rates.
- Social Proof and Trust Indicators: Including social proof elements such as testimonials, reviews, or trust badges can enhance credibility and build trust with visitors. Highlight positive customer experiences and endorsements to reassure potential customers that they are making a reliable and trustworthy decision by engaging with the offer or product.

Elements of a high-converting landing page

A high-converting landing page is designed to maximize the conversion rate and encourage visitors to take the desired action. It is important to optimize key elements to increase the chances of conversion. Here are essential elements of a high-converting landing page:

- Compelling Headline: A strong and compelling

headline immediately captures visitors' attention and entices them to stay on the page. It should clearly communicate the unique value proposition or the benefit of the offer. The headline should be concise, persuasive, and aligned with the messaging throughout the page.

- Clear and Relevant Copy: The copy on a landing page should be concise, persuasive, and easy to understand. It should highlight the benefits of the offer, address visitor pain points, and provide a compelling reason to take action. Use bullet points, subheadings, and short paragraphs to break up the content and make it scannable.

- Persuasive Call-to-Action (CTA): The CTA is a critical element that prompts visitors to take the desired action. It should be visually prominent, using contrasting colors that stand out on the page. The CTA copy should be clear, action-oriented, and compelling, using phrases like "Get Started," "Download Now," or "Sign Up Today." Make sure the CTA button is easily clickable and leads visitors to the next step in the conversion process.

- Lead Capture Form: If the goal of the landing page is to capture leads, the lead capture form should be strategically placed and easy to fill out. Keep the form fields simple and only ask for essential information to minimize friction. Experiment with the number and type of form fields to find the right balance between capturing enough information and reducing form abandonment.

- Visual Elements: Incorporating visually appealing elements such as images, videos, or infographics can enhance engagement and convey information more effectively. Visuals should be relevant to the offer or product and support the overall messaging and value proposition. Use visuals to showcase the benefits or features of the offer and capture visitors' attention.

- Trust Indicators: Building trust is crucial for conversion. Include trust indicators such as customer testimonials, ratings, reviews, security badges, or partner logos to instill confidence and credibility. These indicators assure visitors that their information is safe, the offer is reliable, and others have had positive experiences.
- Clear and Relevant Offer: The offer should be clearly presented and aligned with visitors' expectations. Clearly communicate what visitors will receive in exchange for taking the desired action. Use concise and compelling language to convey the value and benefits of the offer, and consider using urgency or scarcity techniques to create a sense of immediate value.

Creating effective call-to-action (CTA) buttons

Call-to-action (CTA) buttons are critical for guiding visitors to take the desired action on a landing page. Designing effective CTAs can significantly impact conversion rates. Here are key considerations for creating effective CTA buttons:

- Clear and Action-Oriented Language: The CTA button copy should be concise, clear, and action-oriented. Use verbs that prompt visitors to take action, such as "Download," "Sign Up," or "Get

Started." The language should convey a sense of urgency or exclusivity to encourage immediate action.

- Contrasting Visual Design: Make the CTA button visually stand out from the rest of the page by using contrasting colors. Choose a color that contrasts with the background and other elements, making it easily noticeable. The button should be large enough to be easily clickable on both desktop and mobile devices.

- Placement and Visibility: Position the CTA button in a prominent and easily visible location on the landing page. It should be placed above the fold, where visitors can see it without scrolling. Consider using whitespace or directional cues to draw attention to the CTA button and guide visitors' eyes towards it.

- Responsive Design: Ensure that the CTA button is optimized for mobile devices and responsive design. The button should be easily clickable on touchscreens, and the size and placement should adapt to different screen sizes. Test the responsiveness of the CTA button across various devices to ensure a seamless user experience.

- Limited Choices: Minimize distractions and focus visitors' attention on the CTA button by limiting other clickable elements on the page. Avoid including multiple CTAs that may confuse visitors or dilute the main conversion goal. Keeping the choices limited increases the likelihood of visitors clicking on the desired CTA button.

- A/B Testing: Conduct A/B testing to optimize the design and copy of the CTA button. Test different variations, such as color, wording, size, and placement, to identify which combination performs best in terms of conversion rates. A/B testing helps refine the CTA button and improve its effectiveness over time.

Remember, an effective CTA button should be visually appealing, easily clickable, and compelling. It should guide visitors to take the desired action and create a sense of urgency or value. Regularly monitor and analyze the performance of CTAs to make data-driven optimizations for better conversion rates.

Leveraging Content Marketing For Lead Generation

Creating valuable and relevant content

Creating valuable and relevant content is crucial for lead generation. High-quality content attracts and engages potential customers, positioning businesses as trusted authorities and building credibility. Here are key considerations for creating valuable and relevant content:

- Understanding the Target Audience: Start by understanding the needs, preferences, and pain points of the target audience. Conduct market research, analyze customer data, and engage with the target audience to gain insights. This understanding forms the foundation for creating content that resonates with them.
- Providing Educational and Informative Content: Create content that educates and informs the target audience. Address their challenges, answer their questions, and provide solutions to their problems. Valuable content establishes businesses as industry experts and builds trust with potential customers.
- Tailoring Content Formats: Explore various content formats to cater to different preferences and consumption habits. This can include blog articles, videos, infographics, podcasts, case studies, or whitepapers. Adapt the content format to effectively deliver the information and engage the target audience.
- Consistency and Frequency: Consistently produce

and publish content to maintain audience engagement. Develop an editorial calendar and establish a regular content schedule. The frequency of content production should be based on the target audience's preferences and the resources available to create quality content.

- Incorporating Visuals and Multimedia: Visual elements such as images, videos, and graphics enhance the overall appeal and engagement of the content. Use visuals strategically to support the message, convey complex ideas, or evoke emotions. Multimedia elements make the content more shareable and memorable.

- Search Intent Optimization: Align content with the search intent of the target audience. Conduct keyword research to identify relevant keywords and phrases that potential customers are searching for. Optimize content by incorporating these keywords naturally, ensuring the content matches user search queries.

Implementing SEO best practices

Implementing search engine optimization (SEO) best practices is essential for driving organic traffic to a website and generating leads. Here are key considerations for implementing SEO best practices:

- Keyword Research: Conduct comprehensive keyword research to identify relevant keywords and phrases that the target audience is searching for. Use keyword research tools to understand search volumes, competition, and user intent. Incorporate these keywords naturally into website content, including landing pages, blog articles, and meta tags.

- On-Page Optimization: Optimize on-page elements to improve search engine visibility. This includes optimizing title tags, meta descriptions, headers (H1, H2, etc.), and URL structures. Incorporate relevant keywords in these elements while ensuring they accurately describe the content and provide value to users.
- High-Quality Content: Create valuable, informative, and engaging content that aligns with the target audience's needs and preferences. High-quality content attracts backlinks and improves the website's authority and visibility in search results. Regularly update and refresh content to maintain relevance and demonstrate expertise.
- Link Building: Build a strong and authoritative backlink profile by acquiring quality backlinks from reputable websites. Develop relationships with industry influencers, guest post on relevant websites, or create valuable content that naturally attracts backlinks. Focus on earning links from sources that align with the business's industry and target audience.
- Mobile-Friendly Optimization: Optimize the website for mobile devices to provide a seamless user experience. Ensure responsive design, fast loading times, and intuitive navigation on mobile devices. Google considers mobile-friendliness as a ranking factor, so it's crucial to optimize for mobile searchers.
- User Experience and Technical Optimization:

Prioritize user experience by improving website speed, usability, and navigation. Optimize images and multimedia elements to reduce loading times. Ensure proper site structure, clear navigation menus, and logical URL structures. Regularly audit the website for broken links, crawl errors, and other technical issues that may affect search engine visibility.

Using lead magnets and gated content to capture leads

Lead magnets and gated content are effective strategies for capturing leads and encouraging website visitors to provide their contact information. Here are key considerations for using lead magnets and gated content:

- Understanding the Target Audience: Identify the target audience's pain points, needs, and desires. Determine the specific information or resources they would find valuable and be willing to exchange their contact information for.
- Creating Valuable Content: Develop high-quality content that addresses the target audience's pain points or offers a solution to their problems. This content can take the form of e-books, whitepapers, guides, checklists, templates, exclusive reports, or access to webinars or courses. The content should be valuable, actionable, and provide immediate benefits to potential customers.
- Implementing Gated Content: Gate the valuable content behind a lead capture form to encourage visitors to provide their contact information. The form should ask for essential information, such as name and email address, to minimize friction.

Clearly communicate the value of the content and explain why visitors should provide their information.

- Promoting the Lead Magnet: Actively promote the lead magnet or gated content across various marketing channels. Use compelling copy and visuals to highlight the benefits and value of the content. Leverage social media, email marketing, blog posts, and paid advertising to reach the target audience and drive traffic to the landing page where the lead magnet is offered.
- Follow-Up and Nurturing: Once visitors provide their contact information, it's essential to have an effective follow-up and lead nurturing strategy in place. Use marketing automation tools to send personalized email sequences, deliver additional valuable content, and guide leads through the sales funnel.
- Testing and Optimization: Continuously test and optimize lead magnets and gated content to improve conversion rates. Experiment with different formats, titles, visuals, and form fields to find the most effective combination. Monitor analytics and track conversion metrics to make data-driven decisions and refine the lead generation strategy over time.

By offering valuable content and using gated access to capture leads, businesses can build their email list, establish relationships with potential customers, and nurture them towards becoming loyal customers.

CHAPTER THREE

Harnessing the Power of Social Media

Choosing the right social media platforms

Choosing the right social media platforms is crucial for effective lead generation. Not all social media platforms are suitable for every business or target audience. It's important to identify the platforms where the target audience is most active and likely to engage. Here are key considerations for choosing the right social media platforms:

- Identify Target Audience Demographics: Understand the demographics of the target audience, such as age, gender, location, and interests. Research which social media platforms align with these demographics. For example, Facebook has a broad user base spanning various age groups, while platforms like TikTok and Instagram attract younger audiences.

- Analyze User Behavior and Preferences: Examine how the target audience uses social media and their preferences for consuming content. Some audiences may prefer visual content, making platforms like Instagram or Pinterest suitable. Others may engage more with professional and business-related content, making platforms like LinkedIn a better choice.

- Evaluate Platform Features and Capabilities: Consider the features and capabilities of each social media platform. Some platforms may be more conducive to video content (e.g., YouTube) or provide more opportunities for interactive engagement (e.g., Twitter chats or Instagram stories). Choose platforms that align with the types of content and engagement strategies that work best for the business.
- Competitor Analysis: Assess which social media platforms competitors are using successfully. Analyze their engagement levels, follower growth, and the type of content they share on different platforms. This analysis can provide insights into platforms that resonate with the target audience and help identify opportunities for differentiation.
- Resource and Time Considerations: Evaluate the resources available to effectively manage and maintain an active presence on social media platforms. Consider the time, budget, and manpower required to create content, engage with the audience, and monitor analytics. Choose platforms that align with the available resources and allow for consistent and quality engagement.

Strategies for engaging and growing your social media audience

Engaging and growing your social media audience is essential for lead generation. An active and engaged audience increases the likelihood of capturing leads and driving conversions. Here are strategies to effectively engage and grow your social media audience:

- Consistent and Quality Content: Create and share consistent, valuable, and high-quality content that resonates with the target audience. Provide educational content, entertaining posts, industry news, or behind-the-scenes glimpses to keep the audience engaged. Use a mix of formats (text, images, videos) to cater to different preferences.
- Active Engagement: Actively engage with your audience by responding to comments, messages, and mentions. Initiate conversations, ask questions, and encourage audience participation. Show genuine interest in their opinions and feedback. Engaging with the audience fosters a sense of community and loyalty.
- Use Hashtags Effectively: Utilize relevant hashtags to increase the visibility and discoverability of your content. Research and use popular industry-specific or trending hashtags to expand reach and attract a wider audience. Encourage the audience to use branded hashtags to create user-generated content and foster engagement.
- Collaborations and Influencer Partnerships: Collaborate with influencers, industry experts, or complementary businesses to expand your reach and tap into their existing audience. Partnering with influencers or thought leaders can provide access to a larger and more targeted audience. Consider cross-promotions, guest posting, or joint content creation to leverage their influence.
- Run Contests and Giveaways: Organize contests,

giveaways, or sweepstakes to encourage audience participation and grow your following. Set clear rules and requirements for entry, such as liking, sharing, or commenting on a post. Promote the contest across multiple channels to maximize participation and generate buzz.

- Analyze and Optimize: Regularly analyze social media analytics to gain insights into audience preferences, content performance, and engagement metrics. Identify the types of content that resonate the most and optimize your strategy based on these findings. Experiment with different posting times, content formats, and engagement tactics to continuously improve audience engagement.

Leveraging social media advertising for lead generation

Social media advertising can be a powerful tool for lead generation, allowing businesses to target specific audiences and capture leads effectively. Here are strategies for leveraging social media advertising for lead generation:

- Define Campaign Goals: Clearly define the goals and objectives of the advertising campaign. Is the goal to increase brand awareness, drive traffic to a landing page, or capture leads directly? Defining campaign goals helps determine the appropriate targeting, ad format, and call-to-action (CTA) for maximum lead generation impact.
- Audience Targeting: Utilize the robust targeting options provided by social media platforms to reach the desired audience. Define target demographics, interests, behaviors, and location

to narrow down the audience. Refine targeting based on audience insights and adjust as needed to ensure ads reach the most relevant users.

- Compelling Ad Creative: Develop compelling and visually appealing ad creatives that capture attention and communicate the value proposition effectively. Use captivating visuals, concise copy, and strong CTAs to encourage clicks and conversions. A/B test different ad variations to optimize performance.
- Landing Page Optimization: Ensure that the landing page associated with the social media ad is optimized for lead generation. The landing page should align with the ad's messaging, have a clear and persuasive CTA, and offer a valuable lead magnet or content that encourages visitors to provide their contact information.
- Retargeting: Implement retargeting strategies to reach users who have shown interest in your business but have not converted into leads. Set up pixel tracking or audience lists to retarget these users with relevant ads. Customize the ad messaging based on their previous interactions with your brand to increase the likelihood of conversion.
- Lead Generation Ads and Forms: Utilize social media platforms' lead generation ad formats and forms. These ads allow users to provide their contact information directly within the platform, streamlining the lead capture process. Optimize the form fields and minimize friction to encourage higher conversion rates.
- Tracking and Analytics: Implement tracking

mechanisms such as conversion pixels or UTM parameters to track the performance of social media ads. Monitor key metrics such as impressions, clicks, conversions, and cost per lead. Use this data to optimize campaigns, adjust targeting, and refine ad creatives for better lead generation results.

By strategically leveraging social media advertising, businesses can effectively target their ideal audience, drive traffic to lead generation landing pages, and capture valuable leads. Regularly analyze campaign performance, optimize strategies, and make data-driven decisions to maximize lead generation success.

Email Marketing For Lead Nurturing

Building an effective email list

Building an effective email list is crucial for lead generation and nurturing. An email list allows businesses to directly communicate with potential customers and nurture them towards conversion. Here are strategies for building an effective email list:

- Lead Capture Forms: Place lead capture forms strategically on website landing pages, blog posts, and other relevant pages. The forms should be prominently displayed and clearly communicate the value of subscribing to the email list. Keep the form fields minimal to reduce friction and increase conversion rates.
- Opt-in Incentives: Offer opt-in incentives such as exclusive content, e-books, discounts, or free resources in exchange for subscribing to the email list. These incentives provide value to potential subscribers and motivate them to join the list.
- Content Upgrades: Create content upgrades that are directly related to the content visitors are consuming. Offer additional resources, checklists, or guides that provide deeper insights or actionable tips. Require email addresses to access these content upgrades, thus capturing leads.
- Social Media Promotion: Leverage social media platforms to promote the email list and encourage sign-ups. Use compelling copy, visuals, and clear calls-to-action to drive traffic to the lead capture forms or landing pages. Run targeted ads to reach

specific audiences who are likely to be interested in subscribing.

- Guest Blogging and Partnerships: Write guest blog posts for relevant websites and include a call-to-action within the content to join the email list. Collaborate with complementary businesses or influencers to cross-promote each other's email lists to expand reach and attract new subscribers.

- Webinars and Events: Host webinars or participate in industry events where participants need to register with their email addresses. The value provided by these events can entice participants to join the email list for future updates and valuable content.

- Referral Programs: Implement referral programs that reward current subscribers for referring others to join the email list. Provide incentives or exclusive benefits to both the referrer and the new subscriber. Word-of-mouth marketing can significantly increase the reach and growth of the email list.

- Landing Page Optimization: Optimize landing pages dedicated to capturing email leads. Ensure that the landing pages have a clear value proposition, compelling copy, and an easy-to-use sign-up process. Use A/B testing to refine the landing page design and optimize conversion rates.

Crafting personalized and engaging email campaigns

Crafting personalized and engaging email campaigns is essential for nurturing leads and driving conversions. Personalized emails make subscribers feel valued and increase the likelihood of engagement. Here are strategies for crafting personalized and engaging email campaigns:

- Segmentation: Segment the email list based on relevant criteria such as demographics, interests, or behavior. This allows for targeted and personalized messaging. Tailor email content to each segment's specific needs, preferences, and journey within the sales funnel.
- Personalization: Use personalization tags to address subscribers by name and customize email content based on their preferences or past interactions. Personalization can go beyond just the name and include dynamic content blocks, product recommendations, or customized offers based on their browsing or purchase history.
- Compelling Subject Lines: Create subject lines that capture attention and entice subscribers to open the email. Use personalization, curiosity, urgency, or exclusive offers to make the subject lines compelling. A well-crafted subject line can significantly impact open rates.
- Valuable Content: Provide valuable and relevant content in every email. Offer educational content, industry insights, tips, or exclusive offers that cater to subscribers' interests and needs. Deliver content that solves their problems or addresses pain points, keeping them engaged and eager to open future emails.
- Engaging Visuals: Include visually appealing elements in emails, such as images, videos, or infographics, to make the content more engaging and shareable. Visuals should complement the email content and enhance its impact. Ensure that

- visuals are optimized for different devices and email clients.
- Clear Call-to-Action (CTA): Include a clear and prominent CTA that directs subscribers to take the desired action. Make the CTA stand out with contrasting colors and compelling copy. Use a single, focused CTA per email to avoid overwhelming subscribers with too many choices.
- Automation and Triggered Emails: Set up automated email sequences triggered by specific actions or events, such as welcome emails, abandoned cart reminders, or post-purchase follow-ups. These automated emails provide timely and relevant communication, increasing engagement and conversion rates.
- Testing and Optimization: Continuously test and optimize email campaigns to improve performance. Experiment with different subject lines, email content, visuals, and CTAs to identify what resonates best with subscribers. Analyze open rates, click-through rates, and conversion rates to refine the email strategy over time.

Automating lead nurturing processes

Automating lead nurturing processes helps businesses efficiently and consistently engage with leads, guiding them through the sales funnel. Automation ensures timely and personalized communication, improving lead conversion rates. Here are strategies for automating lead nurturing processes:

- Define Lead Scoring and Qualification Criteria: Establish lead scoring and qualification criteria to determine when leads are ready to move to the next stage of the sales funnel. Assign point values to various actions or behaviors, such as website visits, email opens, or content downloads. Use automation tools to track and assign scores to leads based on their engagement levels.

- Implement Drip Email Campaigns: Set up drip email campaigns to deliver a series of pre-defined emails to leads at specific intervals. These campaigns can provide educational content, showcase product features, address common objections, or offer exclusive promotions. Automate the delivery of these emails based on lead behavior or time triggers.

- Personalize Email Content: Utilize automation tools to personalize email content based on lead behavior, demographics, or interests. Dynamically insert lead-specific information, such as their name, company, or previous interactions, to create a personalized experience. Tailor email content based on lead segmentation and engagement history.

- Behavior-based Triggers: Set up behavior-based triggers that automate actions based on lead interactions. For example, if a lead visits a pricing page multiple times, automatically send a personalized email offering more information or a discount. Triggered actions based on specific lead behaviors allow for timely and relevant communication.

- Lead Handoff to Sales Team: Automate the process of handing off qualified leads to the sales team. Define criteria for when leads are considered sales-ready and automatically notify the appropriate sales representative. Ensure seamless integration between marketing automation and customer relationship management (CRM) systems to facilitate lead handoff.

- Lead Scoring and Nurturing Adjustments: Continuously analyze and refine lead scoring and nurturing processes based on data and feedback. Monitor lead engagement, conversion rates, and sales outcomes to identify areas for improvement. Adjust lead scoring criteria, email sequences, or triggers to optimize lead nurturing efforts.
- Test and Optimize: Conduct A/B testing to optimize automated lead nurturing processes. Test different email sequences, subject lines, content variations, or timing to identify what resonates best with leads. Analyze performance metrics, such as open rates, click-through rates, and conversion rates, to make data-driven improvements.

Automation allows businesses to scale their lead nurturing efforts, deliver consistent messaging, and effectively move leads through the sales funnel. Regularly review and refine automation workflows to ensure they align with changing customer needs and business objectives.

Implementing Effective Lead Capture Forms

Designing optimized lead capture forms

Designing optimized lead capture forms is essential for effective lead generation. A well-designed form can encourage visitors to provide their contact information and increase conversion rates. Here are key considerations for designing optimized lead capture forms:

- Keep it Simple: Keep the form fields minimal and only ask for essential information. Long and complex forms can be off-putting and increase form abandonment rates. Only collect information that is necessary for the initial lead qualification and follow-up.
- Clear and Visible Labels: Use clear and visible labels for each form field. Labels should be placed outside the field or use placeholder text that disappears when users start entering their information. Ensure that the labels are easy to read and distinguishable from the input fields.
- Mobile-Friendly Design: Optimize the form design for mobile devices to provide a seamless user experience. Use responsive design techniques to ensure the form is fully functional and easy to fill out on smaller screens. Consider the use of mobile-specific input types, such as date pickers or numeric keyboards, to enhance usability.
- Error Validation and Messages: Implement real-time error validation to provide immediate feedback to users when they make errors or omit required fields. Highlight the specific fields

with errors and provide clear instructions for correction. Use descriptive error messages that guide users in resolving the issues.

- Progress Indicators: If the form has multiple steps, provide a progress indicator to give users a sense of how much is left and how far they have progressed. This helps manage user expectations and reduces form abandonment.
- Visual Cues and Buttons: Use visual cues, such as arrows or pointers, to guide users through the form and draw attention to important elements. Ensure that the submit button is clearly visible, stands out from other elements, and uses compelling copy to encourage submission.
- Trust and Privacy Assurance: Include trust indicators such as security badges, privacy statements, or links to your privacy policy near the form. This helps reassure users that their information is safe and will be handled securely.
- Form Placement: Place the lead capture form in a prominent and visible location on the webpage. It should be positioned above the fold, where visitors can easily see it without scrolling. Consider using sticky or floating form options to ensure it remains visible as users navigate the page.

Reducing friction and improving form completion rates

Reducing friction and improving form completion rates is essential for maximizing lead generation. Friction refers to any obstacles or challenges that prevent users from completing a form. Here are strategies to reduce friction and improve form completion rates:

- Simplify the Form: Streamline the form by reducing the number of required fields. Minimize the cognitive effort required by users to complete the form. Consider using smart form fields that auto-fill or dynamically adjust based on user inputs.
- Autofill and Prepopulate: Utilize autofill capabilities to prepopulate form fields with known information, such as name, email, or address. This saves users time and reduces the effort required to fill out the form.
- Inline Help and Instructions: Provide clear and concise instructions within the form or beside each field to guide users on what information is required. Use tooltips or inline help text to explain the purpose or format of specific fields.
- Mobile Optimization: Optimize the form for mobile devices to ensure a seamless user experience. Use responsive design techniques, large input fields, and touch-friendly elements. Avoid using small fonts or form fields that are too close together, as they can be challenging to interact with on mobile screens.
- Progress Bar: If the form has multiple steps, display a progress bar to indicate the user's progress and how many steps are remaining. This helps users understand the length of the process and encourages them to continue.
- Social Login Options: Offer social login options, such as signing in with Google or Facebook, to simplify the registration process. This eliminates the need for users to manually enter their information and increases convenience.

- Clear Privacy Policy: Assure users of the privacy and security of their information by including a link to your privacy policy near the form. Transparency regarding data handling and security builds trust and reduces concerns about submitting personal information.
- Test and Optimize: Continuously test and optimize form design, length, and layout to improve conversion rates. Conduct A/B tests with different form variations to identify the most effective design. Analyze metrics such as form abandonment rates, completion rates, and conversion rates to make data-driven improvements.

A/B testing and optimizing form performance

A/B testing and optimizing form performance is crucial for maximizing lead generation. A/B testing involves comparing two or more variations of a form to identify the most effective design. Here are strategies for A/B testing and optimizing form performance:

- Identify Key Elements: Determine the specific elements of the form that you want to test, such as form length, field order, button color, copy, or layout. Focus on one or two elements at a time to accurately assess their impact on form performance.
- Create Variations: Develop multiple versions of the form, each with a single variation in the identified key element(s). For example, create one form with a long format and another with a short format. Ensure that each variation is equally

visible and accessible to users.

- Split Test Allocation: Randomly divide your website traffic between the different form variations. This ensures that each variation is tested with a representative sample of users. Use A/B testing tools or platforms to automate the allocation and measurement of results.
- Define Metrics: Determine the metrics that will be used to measure form performance, such as conversion rate, completion rate, or form abandonment rate. Establish a clear hypothesis for each test and the expected impact on the defined metrics.
- Monitor and Analyze Results: Track and analyze the performance of each form variation using the defined metrics. Collect data on user behavior, engagement, and conversion rates for each variation. Use statistical significance testing to validate the results and ensure they are reliable.
- Implement Successful Variations: Based on the results of the A/B tests, identify the variations that perform better and generate higher conversion rates. Implement the successful variations as the new default form design.
- Iterative Optimization: A/B testing should be an ongoing process of continuous improvement. Regularly test new variations and fine-tune form elements based on user feedback and evolving user preferences. Optimize the form design to maximize conversion rates and lead generation effectiveness.
- Consider User Feedback: Incorporate user feedback and insights into the optimization

process. Monitor user comments, survey responses, and feedback channels to identify areas of improvement. User feedback can provide valuable insights into pain points, usability issues, or suggestions for enhancing the form experience.

Remember, A/B testing and optimization should be data-driven processes. Use the insights gained from each test to make informed decisions and continuously refine the form design. Regularly monitor form performance and conduct periodic A/B tests to ensure ongoing optimization and improvement.

CHAPTER FOUR

Utilizing Marketing
Automation Tools

Introduction to marketing automation

Marketing automation refers to the use of software platforms and technologies to automate marketing tasks and workflows. It streamlines and automates repetitive marketing activities, allowing businesses to efficiently engage with leads, nurture relationships, and drive conversions. Marketing automation combines various tools and strategies to deliver personalized, timely, and relevant messages to prospects and customers. It enables businesses to scale their marketing efforts, improve efficiency, and achieve better marketing outcomes.

Marketing automation encompasses a range of capabilities, including lead generation, lead nurturing, email marketing, customer segmentation, campaign management, social media marketing, analytics, and more. By automating these processes, businesses can optimize their marketing efforts, save time and resources, and deliver a more personalized and targeted customer experience.

Benefits of marketing automation for lead generation

Marketing automation offers numerous benefits for lead generation. Here are some key adgeneratio

- Improved Lead Quality: Marketing automation enables businesses to implement lead scoring and lead qualification processes. By tracking lead behavior, engagement, and demographic data, businesses can assign scores to leads based on their level of interest and readiness to purchase. This helps prioritize and focus efforts on the most qualified leads, increasing the chances of conversion.
- Streamlined Lead Nurturing: Marketing automation allows businesses to deliver personalized and targeted content to leads at different stages of the buying journey. Automated email workflows and drip campaigns can be set up to deliver relevant content based on lead behavior and interests. This helps nurture leads, build relationships, and move them closer to making a purchase.
- Increased Efficiency and Productivity: Automating repetitive marketing tasks frees up time and resources, allowing marketing teams to focus on strategic activities and high-value tasks. By automating workflows, businesses can streamline processes, reduce manual effort, and improve overall marketing efficiency.
- Personalization and Customer Segmentation: Marketing automation enables businesses to segment their audience based on demographics, behavior, interests, or other criteria. This segmentation allows for more personalized and targeted messaging, improving the relevance

and effectiveness of marketing campaigns. By delivering tailored content to specific segments, businesses can enhance engagement and increase conversion rates.

- Enhanced Lead Tracking and Analytics: Marketing automation tools provide comprehensive tracking and analytics capabilities. Businesses can track lead interactions, measure campaign performance, and gain insights into the effectiveness of marketing efforts. This data helps identify areas for improvement, optimize campaigns, and make data-driven decisions.

- Multi-Channel Campaign Management: Marketing automation platforms facilitate multi-channel marketing campaigns, including email marketing, social media marketing, and website personalization. Businesses can manage and coordinate their marketing efforts across different channels, ensuring consistent messaging and optimizing the customer experience.

- Improved Alignment of Sales and Marketing: Marketing automation helps align sales and marketing teams by providing shared visibility into lead activity and engagement. It enables better communication, collaboration, and lead handoff between teams, fostering a more seamless and efficient sales process.

- Scalability and Growth: Marketing automation is highly scalable, allowing businesses to handle increasing lead volumes and grow their customer base without significant manual effort. Automated workflows, lead scoring, and nurturing processes can be easily scaled to accommodate larger audiences, ensuring consistent and effective lead generation.

Selecting and implementing the right marketing automation tools

Selecting and implementing the right marketing automation tools is essential for successful lead generation. Here are key considerations when choosing and implementing marketing automation tools:

- Define Your Objectives and Requirements: Clearly define your marketing automation objectives and the specific features and functionalities you require. Consider your current marketing processes, lead generation goals, budget, and integration requirements. This will help you evaluate and choose the right tool that aligns with your business needs.
- Research and Evaluate Multiple Tools: Conduct thorough research and evaluate multiple marketing automation tools. Consider factors such as ease of use, scalability, integration capabilities, customer support, pricing, and reputation. Read reviews, seek recommendations, and compare features to ensure the tool meets your requirements.
- Integration with Existing Systems: Assess the compatibility and integration capabilities of the marketing automation tool with your existing systems, such as CRM software, customer databases, or content management systems.

Seamless integration ensures smooth data flow and enables a unified view of customer interactions.

- User-Friendliness and Training: Consider the ease of use and the learning curve associated with the marketing automation tool. Evaluate the availability of training resources, documentation, and customer support to help your team effectively adopt and utilize the tool.

- Scalability and Growth Potential: Choose a marketing automation tool that can scale with your business and accommodate future growth. Consider the pricing structure, licensing models, and flexibility to handle increasing lead volumes and expanding marketing efforts.

- Data Security and Compliance: Ensure that the marketing automation tool adheres to industry standards for data security and compliance, especially if you handle sensitive customer information. Evaluate the tool's data protection measures, encryption capabilities, and compliance with privacy regulations, such as GDPR or CCPA.

- Implementation and Onboarding Support: Evaluate the implementation process and onboarding support offered by the marketing automation vendor. Consider the availability of training, implementation assistance, and ongoing support to ensure a smooth transition and successful utilization of the tool.

- Measure Success and Iterate: Once the marketing automation tool is implemented, establish key performance indicators (KPIs) to measure its effectiveness. Monitor metrics such as lead generation, conversion rates, engagement rates, and campaign performance. Continuously analyze the results, make data-driven adjustments, and iterate to optimize your lead generation efforts

Selecting the right marketing automation tool and effectively implementing it can significantly enhance lead generation efforts. Take the time to evaluate different options, consider your business needs, and ensure a smooth implementation process to maximize the benefits of marketing automation.

Analyzing And Measuring Lead Generation Success

Defining key performance indicators (KPIs)

Defining key performance indicators (KPIs) is crucial for measuring the effectiveness of lead generation efforts. KPIs are measurable metrics that reflect the performance and progress towards specific goals. By establishing KPIs, businesses can track and evaluate the success of their lead generation strategies. Here are steps to define effective KPIs:

- Identify Goals: Clearly define the goals of your lead generation efforts. These goals could include increasing the number of leads, improving lead quality, boosting conversion rates, or enhancing overall revenue. Align your KPIs with these goals to ensure they reflect the desired outcomes.
- Quantify Success: Determine how success will be quantified for each goal. For example, if the goal is to increase the number of leads, the KPI could be the number of new leads generated per month. If the goal is to improve conversion rates, the KPI could be the percentage of leads that convert into customers.
- Be Specific and Measurable: Ensure that each KPI is specific and measurable. Avoid vague or subjective KPIs. For example, instead of setting a goal to "increase website traffic," a more specific KPI would be to "increase website traffic by 20% over the next quarter."
- Align with Business Objectives: Ensure that your

chosen KPIs align with your overall business objectives. Consider how the KPIs contribute to the broader goals of the organization and impact its growth and success.

- Set Realistic Targets: Set realistic targets for each KPI based on historical data, industry benchmarks, or growth projections. Targets should be challenging yet attainable, providing motivation for improvement without being unattainable.
- Track Progress Over Time: Continuously track and monitor the performance of each KPI over time. Regularly analyze the data to identify trends, patterns, and areas for improvement. Adjust targets or KPIs as needed based on the insights gained from the analysis.
- Communicate and Align: Clearly communicate the defined KPIs to the relevant stakeholders, including marketing teams, sales teams, and executives. Ensure that everyone understands the importance of each KPI and how it contributes to the overall business objectives. Align efforts and strategies around achieving the defined KPIs.

Tracking and analyzing lead generation metrics

Tracking and analyzing lead generation metrics is essential for understanding the effectiveness of your lead generation strategies and making data-driven decisions. By monitoring key metrics, businesses can identify areas for improvement, optimize their lead generation efforts, and maximize conversions. Here are key lead generation metrics to track and analyze:

- Conversion Rate: Measure the percentage of leads that convert into customers. This metric indicates the effectiveness of your lead generation and nurturing efforts in driving actual revenue.
- Cost per Lead: Calculate the average cost incurred to generate a single lead. This metric helps evaluate the efficiency and cost-effectiveness of your lead generation campaigns and channels.
- Lead Quality: Assess the quality of generated leads by analyzing factors such as lead source, demographic data, behavior, or engagement metrics. This metric helps identify the sources and characteristics of high-quality leads, enabling you to refine targeting and lead qualification strategies.
- Lead Velocity: Measure the speed at which leads move through the sales funnel. This metric provides insights into the efficiency of your lead nurturing and conversion processes. A faster lead velocity indicates effective lead nurturing and a shorter sales cycle.
- Website Traffic: Monitor the number of visitors to your website and specific landing pages. This metric helps assess the effectiveness of your website and content in attracting and engaging potential leads.
- Click-Through Rate (CTR): Measure the percentage of leads who click on links or calls-to-action in your emails, ads, or landing pages. CTR indicates the level of engagement and interest among your leads.
- Landing Page Conversion Rate: Calculate the percentage of visitors who complete a desired

action, such as filling out a form or subscribing to a newsletter, on your landing page. This metric evaluates the effectiveness of your landing page design and optimization in capturing leads.

- Email Open and Click Rates: Track the percentage of recipients who open your emails and the percentage who click on links within the emails. These metrics indicate the effectiveness of your email campaigns in capturing attention and generating engagement.
- Social Media Engagement: Monitor engagement metrics such as likes, shares, comments, and followers on social media platforms. This metric provides insights into the reach and impact of your social media lead generation efforts.
- Return on Investment (ROI): Evaluate the overall return on investment of your lead generation campaigns. Compare the revenue generated against the costs incurred to measure the financial success of your efforts.

Strategies for continuous improvement and optimization

Continuous improvement and optimization are essential for maximizing lead generation effectiveness. By regularly analyzing data, identifying areas for improvement, and implementing targeted strategies, businesses can optimize their lead generation efforts and achieve better results. Here are strategies for continuous improvement and optimization:

- Analyze Data and Insights: Regularly analyze lead generation metrics and performance data to identify patterns, trends, and areas for improvement. Use analytics tools and platforms to gain insights into the effectiveness of different campaigns, channels, and strategies.

- Conduct A/B Testing: Implement A/B testing to compare different variations of landing pages, forms, email content, or calls-to-action. Test one element at a time and analyze the impact on lead generation metrics. Use the results to make data-driven decisions and optimize your approach.
- Optimize Landing Pages and Forms: Continuously optimize your landing pages and lead capture forms based on user behavior and feedback. Test different layouts, messaging, visuals, and form fields to increase conversion rates and minimize friction.
- Refine Targeting and Segmentation: Continuously evaluate and refine your target audience and segmentation strategies. Analyze lead data and feedback to identify specific segments that respond well to your messaging and offers. Tailor your lead generation efforts to cater to these segments.
- Nurture and Engage Leads: Implement effective lead nurturing strategies to keep leads engaged and guide them through the sales funnel. Provide personalized and valuable content, address pain points, and deliver timely and relevant messages based on lead behavior and interests.
- Improve User Experience: Focus on enhancing the user experience across all touchpoints of your lead generation process. Optimize website navigation, page load times, mobile responsiveness, and overall usability. Ensure a

seamless and intuitive experience for potential leads.

- Monitor Competitors: Keep an eye on your competitors' lead generation strategies and campaigns. Analyze their tactics, messaging, and targeting to gain insights and identify potential areas for improvement or differentiation.
- Seek Feedback and Learn from Customers: Encourage feedback from your customers and leads to understand their preferences, pain points, and experiences with your lead generation efforts. Leverage customer feedback to iterate and enhance your strategies.
- Stay Updated with Industry Trends: Stay abreast of the latest industry trends, technologies, and best practices in lead generation. Attend industry events, read relevant publications, and follow thought leaders to gain insights and inspiration for optimizing your strategies.
- Foster Collaboration and Alignment: Foster collaboration and alignment between marketing and sales teams. Regularly communicate, share insights, and collaborate on lead generation strategies and tactics. Create a feedback loop to ensure continuous improvement based on sales feedback and lead conversion data.

By consistently implementing these strategies for continuous improvement and optimization, businesses can refine their lead generation efforts, increase conversions, and drive business growth. Continuously monitor, measure, and adapt your strategies based on data-driven insights to stay ahead of the competition and maximize the potential of your lead generation activities.

Lead Generation Best Practices And Case Studies

Expert tips and industry best practices

To optimize lead generation in web-based business arrangements, it's valuable to consider expert tips and industry best practices. Here are some key recommendations:

- Define Your Target Audience: Clearly identify and understand your target audience's demographics, interests, pain points, and behaviors. This knowledge allows you to tailor your lead generation strategies to effectively engage and convert your ideal customers.
- Create Compelling and Valuable Content: Develop high-quality content that is valuable, relevant, and addresses your audience's needs and pain points. Whether it's blog posts, videos, e-books, or webinars, focus on providing informative and engaging content that establishes your expertise and builds trust with potential leads.
- Optimize for Search Engines: Implement search engine optimization (SEO) techniques to ensure your content ranks well in search engine results. Conduct keyword research, optimize meta tags and descriptions, and create high-quality backlinks to improve your website's visibility and drive organic traffic.
- Utilize Social Media Channels: Choose the social media platforms that align with your target audience's preferences and behavior. Create a

strong social media presence, engage with your audience, share valuable content, and leverage paid advertising to expand your reach and generate leads.

- Implement Conversion Rate Optimization (CRO) Strategies: Continuously optimize your landing pages, forms, and call-to-action buttons to improve conversion rates. Conduct A/B testing, experiment with different elements and layouts, and analyze user behavior to identify areas for improvement and enhance user experience.
- Nurture Leads with Email Marketing: Develop a comprehensive email marketing strategy to nurture leads and guide them through the sales funnel. Personalize your emails, segment your audience, and automate email sequences to deliver relevant and timely messages that drive engagement and conversions.
- Leverage Marketing Automation: Implement marketing automation tools to streamline and automate repetitive marketing tasks, such as email campaigns, lead scoring, and lead nurturing. Automation improves efficiency, allows for personalized communication, and enables effective lead management.
- Monitor and Analyze Data: Continuously track and analyze lead generation metrics to gain insights into the performance of your strategies. Monitor conversion rates, website traffic, engagement metrics, and ROI. Use data to identify patterns, adjust tactics, and make data-driven decisions for ongoing optimization.

Case studies highlighting successful lead generation campaigns

Case studies highlighting successful lead generation campaigns can provide valuable insights and inspiration for optimizing your own strategies. Here are a few examples of successful lead generation campaigns:

- Company X: Company X implemented a content marketing strategy focused on creating in-depth, educational blog posts and resources. They optimized their content for SEO, shared it on social media, and collected email addresses through gated content. This approach generated a steady flow of high-quality leads, resulting in a significant increase in conversions and revenue.
- Company Y: Company Y launched a targeted Facebook advertising campaign to reach their ideal audience. They utilized detailed audience targeting, compelling ad creative, and a well-designed landing page with an optimized lead capture form. By continuously monitoring and optimizing their campaign, they achieved a high conversion rate and a significant boost in lead generation.
- Company Z: Company Z implemented a personalized email marketing campaign to nurture leads and drive conversions. They segmented their email list based on user behavior and preferences, and created tailored email sequences. By delivering relevant content and offers to their leads, they achieved higher engagement, increased open rates, and improved conversion rates.

These case studies demonstrate the importance of targeted strategies, valuable content, optimization, and continuous monitoring and optimization to achieve successful lead generation campaigns.

Lessons learned and actionable takeaways

From the examples and experiences shared in the case studies, here are some actionable takeaways and lessons learned for optimizing lead generation:

- Audience Focus: Prioritize understanding your target audience's needs, preferences, and behaviors. Tailor your strategies and content to address their pain points and provide value.
- Valuable Content: Create high-quality, valuable content that educates and engages your audience. Focus on providing solutions, answering their questions, and establishing yourself as a trusted authority.
- Optimization and Testing: Continuously optimize your landing pages, forms, ads, and emails to improve conversion rates. Conduct A/B testing, track performance metrics, and make data-driven decisions for ongoing improvement.
- Personalization and Segmentation: Implement personalization and segmentation strategies to deliver targeted and relevant messaging to your leads. This enhances engagement and increases the likelihood of conversion.
- Multi-Channel Approach: Utilize multiple channels, such as content marketing, social media, email marketing, and paid advertising, to reach your audience effectively. Create a cohesive

and integrated approach that maximizes your visibility and engagement.

- Data Analysis and Tracking: Monitor and analyze lead generation metrics to gain insights into the performance of your strategies. Use this data to identify trends, optimize campaigns, and make informed decisions for continuous improvement.
- Agile Approach: Be open to experimentation, adapt quickly to changing trends and audience preferences, and iterate your strategies based on results. Embrace an agile approach that allows you to continuously learn, optimize, and evolve your lead generation efforts.
- By applying these lessons learned and taking actionable steps, businesses can optimize their lead generation strategies and drive consistent, high-quality leads for their web-based business arrangements.

CONCLUSION

In conclusion, "The Wishpond Lead Generation Guide" serves as a comprehensive and indispensable resource for anyone seeking to unlock the power of effective lead generation. Throughout this book, we have explored a myriad of proven strategies, tactics, and techniques to help you attract, engage, and convert your target audience into valuable leads.

By delving into the core concepts of lead generation, we have provided you with a solid foundation upon which to build your marketing campaigns. From crafting compelling offers and optimizing landing pages to leveraging social media and email marketing, we have covered the essential components necessary for successful lead generation.

Moreover, we have emphasized the importance of understanding your audience and their unique needs, ensuring that you tailor your approach to resonate with them effectively. By employing customer-centric strategies and implementing data-driven insights, you can forge deeper connections with your prospects, fostering trust and loyalty along the way.

Throughout this journey, we have also emphasized the significance of continuous improvement and experimentation. Lead generation is an evolving landscape, and it requires a willingness to adapt, test, and refine your strategies. By embracing a growth mindset and staying abreast of emerging trends, you can stay ahead of the curve and maintain a competitive edge.

Remember, lead generation is not a one-time event but an ongoing process that requires dedication, creativity, and persistence. The insights shared in this guide will serve as valuable tools to help you navigate the ever-changing digital marketing landscape, enabling you to generate a steady stream of high-quality leads and propel your business towards success.

Now armed with this knowledge, it is up to you to take action and implement these strategies effectively. Embrace the power of Wishpond and the principles outlined in this guide to transform your lead generation efforts and unlock a world of possibilities for your business.

As you embark on this exciting journey, may "The Wishpond Lead Generation Guide" be your trusted companion, inspiring you to reach new heights, make meaningful connections, and achieve your business objectives. Here's to your continued growth and prosperity. Happy lead generation!